you played 8/19/00 as my Maid of Honor as you offered words of encouragement, helping hands, unconditional love & eternal friendship.

With love & gratitude from the bottom of my heart,

Tara

Beverly Clark's
For My Bridesmaid

Beverly Clark's
For My Bridesmaid

Running Press
PHILADELPHIA · LONDON

A Running Press Miniature Edition™
© 1999 by Beverly Clark

All rights reserved under the Pan-American and International Copyright Conventions

Printed in China

This book may not be reproduced in whole or in part, in any form or by any means, electronic or mechanical, including photocopying, recording, or any information storage and retrieval system now known or hereafter invented, without written permission from the publisher.

The proprietary trade dress, including the size and format, of this Running Press Miniature Edition™ is the property of Running Press. It may not be used or reproduced without the express written permission of Running Press.

For My Bridesmaid is derived from Beverly Clark's **Weddings: A Celebration**.

Library of Congress Cataloging-in-Publication Number 98-68471

ISBN 0-7624-0627-5

This book may be ordered by mail from the publisher. Please include $1.00 for postage and handling.

But try your bookstore first!

Running Press Book Publishers
125 South Twenty-second Street
Philadelphia, Pennsylvania 19103-4399

Visit us on the web!
www.runningpress.com

Contents

Introduction . . . 6

Eternal Friendship . . . 13

Words of Encouragement . . . 43

Helping Hands . . . 69

Unconditional Love . . . 97

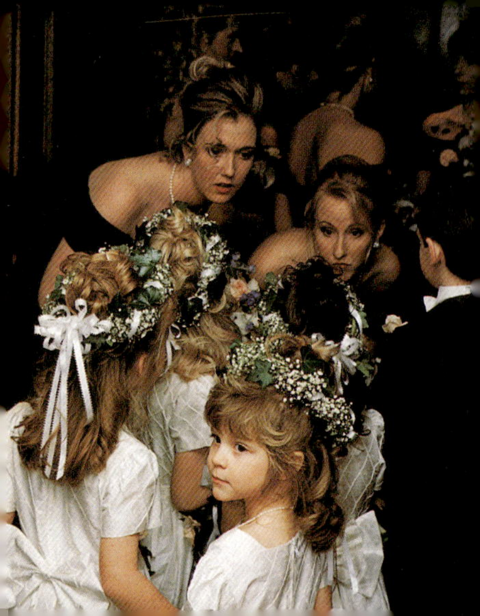

Introduction

When she first learns of her impending nuptials, the bride-to-be is often anxious to ask her closest friends to stand up for her at her wedding. These people have proven themselves to be true friends. They held her hand when she got her first failing grade in school, nursed her wounds when she was passed up for that promotion at work, and ate pints of ice cream with her when her former boyfriend turned out to be a complete jerk. Sharing her joy with these friends makes her own happiness even more profound.

Every former bridesmaid, however, knows that the job can be a thankless one. The bride is preoccupied with her fiancé, wedding plans, and future in-laws, while the bridesmaids address envelopes for hours on end and offer emotional support on demand. To top that off, the bridesmaids' dresses are often pink or lavender gowns that make the attendants look like escapees from a debutante ball.

Still, we can't imagine declining her offer. We want to throw her a shower and hold her bouquet. She is our friend, and nothing makes us happier than seeing her happy. While her husband-to-be is her lover and soul mate, we are her sisters. We understand her because we know what it's like to be her.

Collected here are a few thoughts celebrating the special role that our bridesmaids play in our lives. Share these sentiments with other beleaguered souls who may need to be reminded why they should be honored and proud to claim the title: bridesmaid.

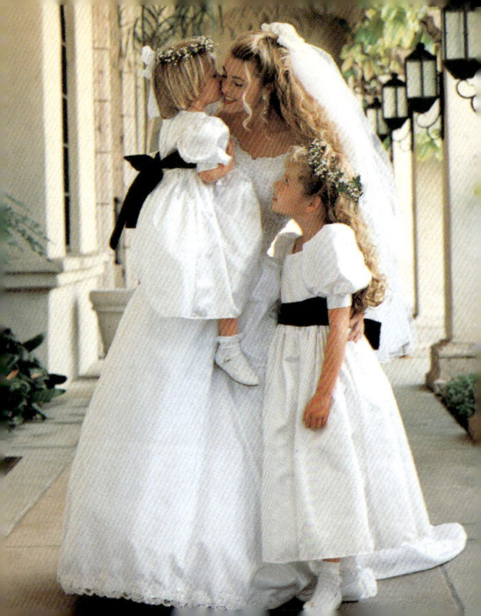

Eternal
Friendship

From ancient Rome through the Middle Ages, bridesmaids had two purposes: to protect the bride from evil spirits . . . and to stand as witness for her. To protect women from being married against their will, societies required at least two witnesses who would attest to the bride's willingness, one of whom was her closest friend, her maid of honor.

Beverly Clark
American bridal authority and writer

The silver friend knows your present and the gold friend knows all of your past dirt and glories. Once in a blue moon there's someone who knows it all, someone who knows and accepts you unconditionally, someone who's there for life.

Jill McCorkle
American writer

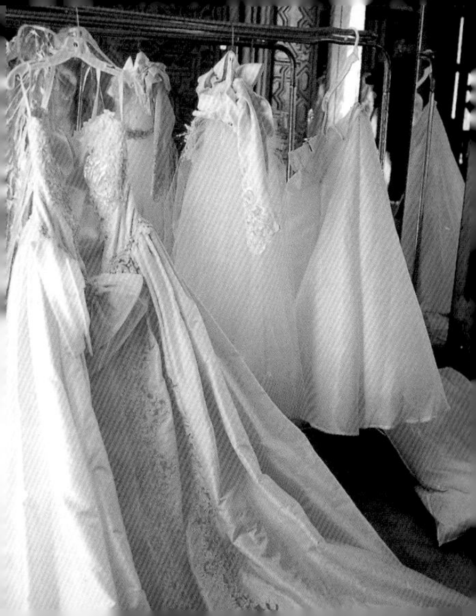

The truth is friendship is every bit
as sacred and eternal as marriage.

Katherine Mansfield (1888–1923)
New Zealand-born British writer

From the rocking horse to the rocking chair, friendship keeps teaching us about being human.

Letty Cottin Pogrebin
American writer

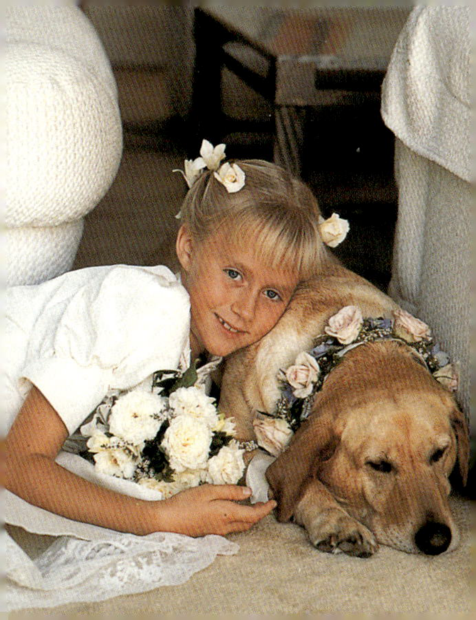

There are some friends you know you will have for the rest of your life. You're welded together by love, trust, respect . . .

from the 1993 Film *Peter's Friends*

Love is like the wild
    rose-briar;

Friendship like the holly-tree.

The holly is dark when
    the rose-briar blooms,

But which will bloom most
    constantly?

        Emily Brönte (1818–1848)
        English writer

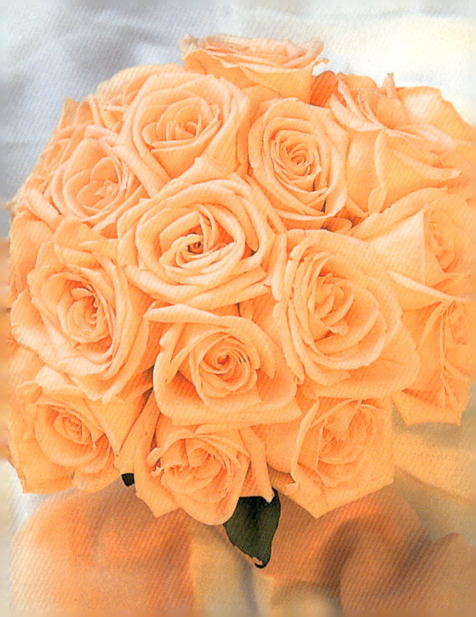

My friends are my estate.

Emily Dickinson (1830–1886)
American poet

Constant use had not worn ragged the fabric of their friendship.

                Dorothy Parker (1893–1967)
                American writer

Great friendships with women are some of life's most difficult and caring intimacies. If I work harder at them, I hope to have them forever.

Wendy Wasserstein
American playwright

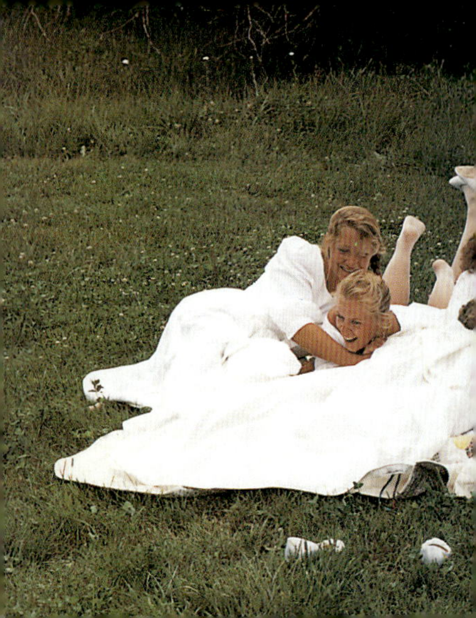

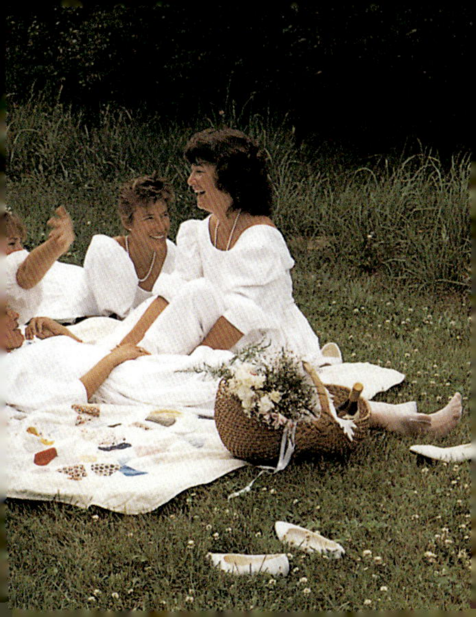

Yes'm, old friends is always best, 'less you can catch a new one that's fit to make an old one out of.

Sarah Orne Jewett (1848–1909)
American writer

...there's no understanding the future without the present, and no understanding where we are now without a glance, at least, to where we have been.

Joyce Maynard
American writer

Females, beginning with my sisters, had been my most loyal, most satisfactory companions.

> Luanne Rice
> American writer

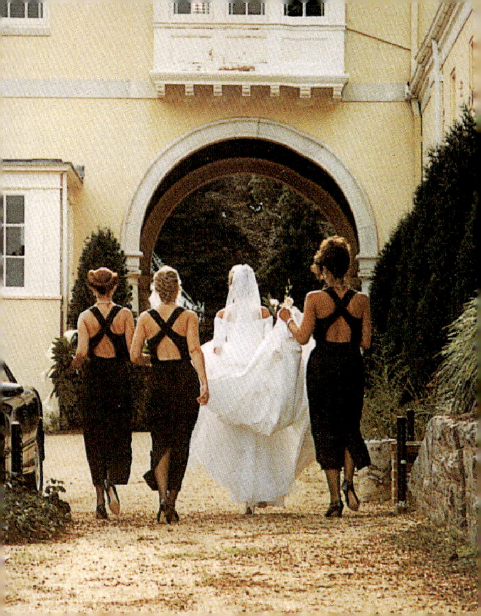

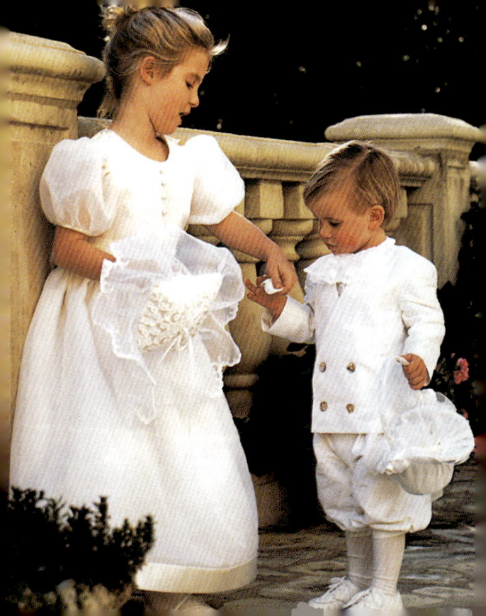

When she kissed my cheek she whispered "sister-love" in my ear, so softly I wasn't sure I'd heard it until I looked in her eyes.

> Jewelle Gomez
> American writer

. . . one's sister is a part of one's essential self, an eternal presence of one's heart and soul and memory.

> Susan Cahill
> American writer

I have all kinds of thoughts and feelings about her, but first and last we are two kindred bodies.

Kennedy Fraser
American writer

The tradition of flower girls goes back many centuries, and it's easy to see why—they're irresistible.

Beverly Clark
American wedding authority
and writer

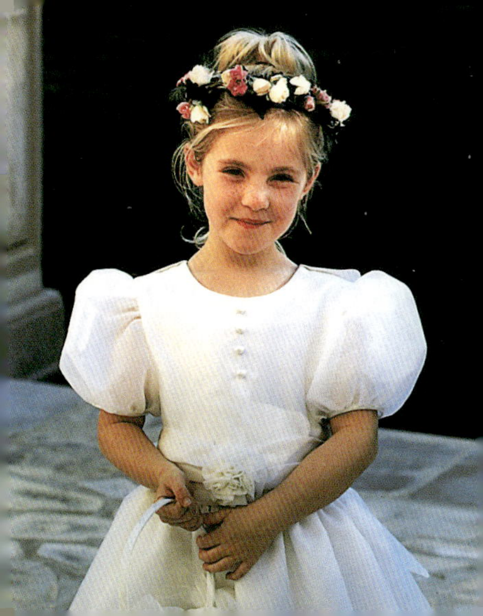

To have a loving relationship with a sister is not simply to have a buddy or a confidante—it is to have a soul mate for life.

Victoria Secunda
American writer

I remember slumber parties . . . where no slumber was involved, only secrets and dares. . . . I remember lunches that I never wanted to end. Birthdays that glowed. From all those times, those eternal sacred moments of my life strung together inside me, pearl by pearl, I learned what it is to be happy.

Michele Weldon
American journalist

Each one of these women is unique and special to me and has played a significant role in my life. I would like to thank each of them for being such good friends to me over the years.

> Kellie Speed
> American writer

O Bridesmaid, ere the
    happy knot was tied,

Thine eyes as wept that
    they could hardly see;

Thy sister smiled and said,
    "No tears form!

A happy bridesmaid makes
    a happy bride."

              Alfred, Lord Tennyson
                  (1809–1892)
                   English poet

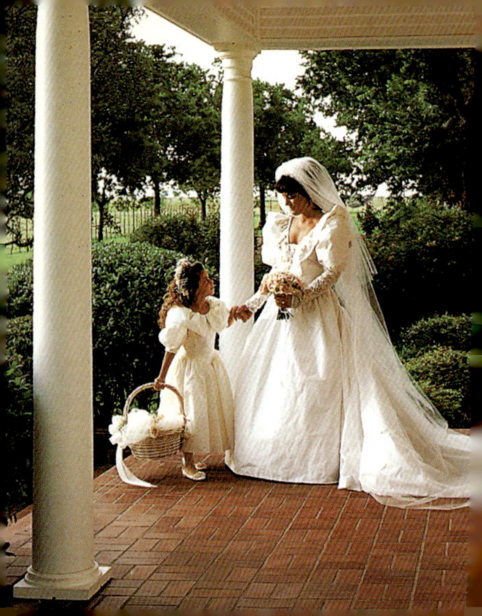

Words of Encouragement

I think there is a thread that runs through each friendship and keeps it going, no words necessary. Each knows what the other knows about him, through good times and bad.

Lauren Bacall
American actress

There was a definite process by which one made people into friends, and it involved talking to them and listening to them for hours at a time.

Rebecca West (1892–1983)
English writer

After an acquaintance of ten minutes many women will exchange confidences that a man would not reveal to a lifelong friend.

Page Smith
American historian

Intimacies between women
often go backwards, beginning in
revelations and ending in small
talk without loss of esteem.

> Elizabeth Bowen
> American writer

There were equal measures of comfort and amusement in our communications; I think it is safe to say that we delighted in one another. She used to laugh at my stories until she wept, and I tried to take her sound advice to heart.

> Jane Hamilton
> American writer

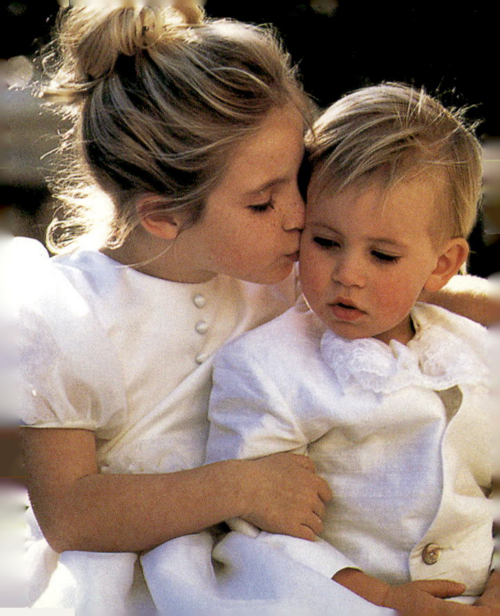

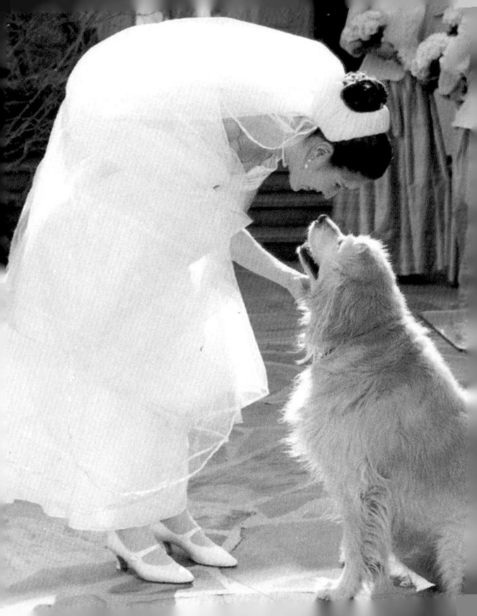

A friend is a person who tells you all the nice things you always knew about yourself.

                        Anonymous

Being a friend means mastering the art of timing. There is a time for silence. A time to let go and allow people to hurl themselves into their own history. And a time to pick up the pieces when it's all over.

Gloria Naylor
American writer

... how rare it is to be able to get into that kind of conversation with an old friend that goes on for years and years and just continues underneath everything.

> Marge Piercy
> American writer

I always felt that the great high privilege, relief, and comfort of friendship was that one had to explain nothing.

Katherine Mansfield (1888–1923)
New Zealand-born British writer

Oh, the comfort, the inexpressible comfort of feeling safe with a person, having neither to weigh thoughts nor measure words, but pouring them all right out, just as they are, chaff and grain together; certain that a faithful hand will take and sift them, keep what is worth keeping, and then with the breath of kindness blow the rest away.

Dinah Maria Mulock Craik (1826–1887)
English writer

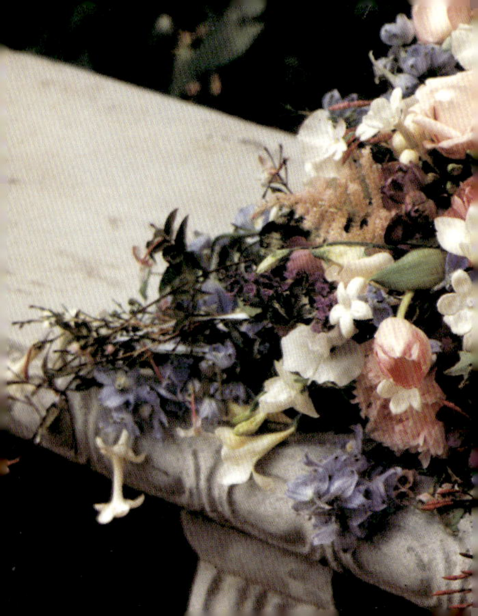

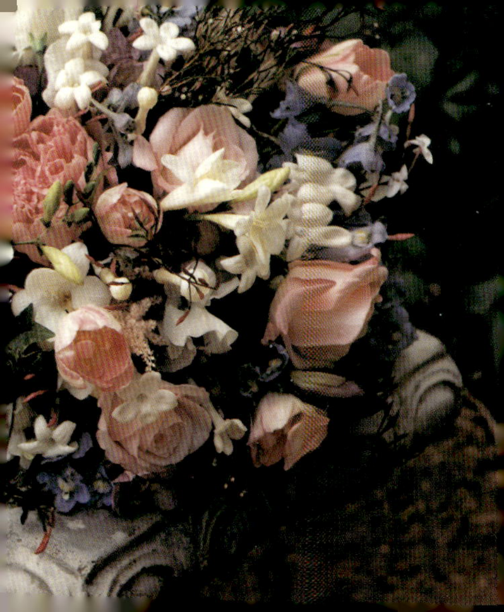

Above all else, lovers want to be together. Barring that, they most enjoy two other pastimes: thinking, daydreaming, or brooding over their beloved; and confiding, confessing, or speaking obsessively about their love to an intimate friend....

                      Ethel Spector Person
              American psychiatrist and writer

What a luxury it was to spend time with old friends with whom it was okay to talk about nothing much.

Lisa Alther
American writer

...we have been talking, as old friends should talk, about nothing, about everything.

> Lillian Hellman (1906–1984)
> American writer

Silences make the real conversations between friends. Not the saying but the never needing to say is what counts.

> Margaret Lee Runbeck
> Canadian writer

A friend is someone you can be alone with and have nothing to do and not be able to think of anything to say and be comfortable in the silence.

Sheryl Condie
American writer

A friendship can weather most silly things and thrive in thin soil—but it needs a little mulch of letters and phone calls and small silly presents every so often—just to save it from drying out completely.

Pam Brown
Australian poet

Unbosom yourself. . . . Trouble shared is trouble halved.

> Dorothy Sayers (1893–1957)
> English writer

Bridal Table

To communicate

with your friend doesn't mean you have to have an answer for their troubles. You just have to be aware of them and share with them and care for them.

Robyn Freedman Spizman
American teacher,
lecturer, and writer

...the responsibilities of friendship?...To talk. And to listen.

> Rosie Thomas
> Welsh writer

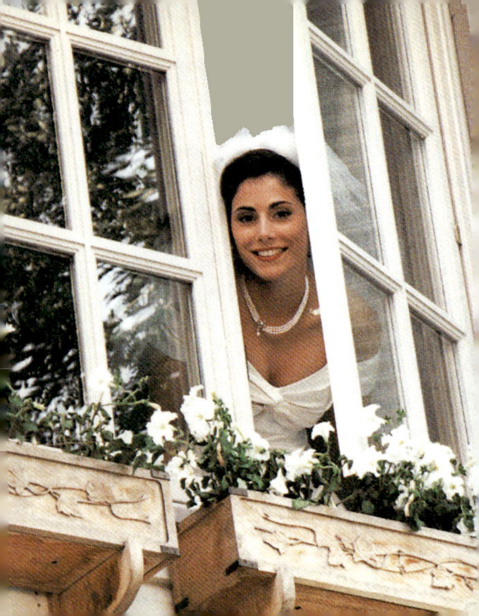

Helping Hands

Your wedding day may be the closest you ever come to starring in an elaborate production. Like any leading lady, you'll depend on your supporting players for encouragement and inspiration.

> Beverly Clark
> American wedding authority
> and writer

Ladies of honor, worthy wives

of worthy husbands, old in love

Escort her in . . .

> Gaius Valerius Catullus
> (c. 84 B.C.–c. 54 B.C.)

Close friends contribute to our personal growth. They also contribute to our personal pleasure, making the music sound sweeter, the wine taste richer, the laughter ring louder because they are there.

Judith Viorst
American writer

It seems to me that trying to live without friends is like milking a bear to get cream for your morning coffee. It is a whole lot of trouble, and then not worth much after you get it.

Zora Neale Hurston (1903–1960)
American writer

Through knowing her I became a better person, and she said the same of me.

Amanda Cross
American writer

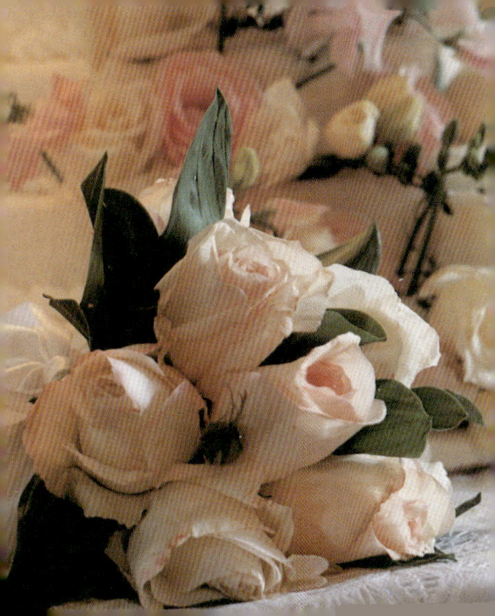

Best friends . . . show us we have separate lives. They offer us affection solely for who we are, surprise us with the scope of another's existence. . . .

> Valerie Shultz
> American writer

Blessed is the influence of one true, human soul on another.

> George Eliot
> [Mary Ann Evans] (1819–1880)
> English writer

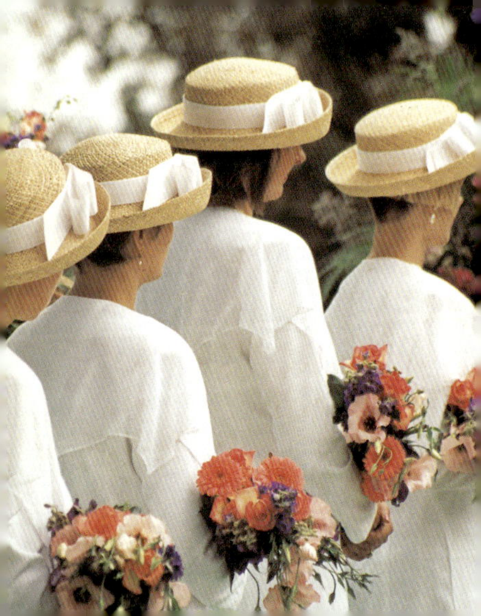

I can trust my friends.
These people force me to examine,
encourage me to grow.

> Cher
> American singer
> and actress

I found myself thinking of Lily and Margo. They understood me. I was always at my best when I was with them because they knew what to look for.

> Luanne Rice
> American writer

I guess I have been hiding. . . .
Most of my life, mostly from myself.
But you . . . you keep blowing my
cover! You keep showing me myself!

> Elizabeth Cunningham
> American writer

Each friend represents a world in us, a world possibly not born until they arrive, and it is only by this meeting that a new world is born.

> Anaïs Nin (1903–1977)
> French-born American writer

Friendship...can take different forms. It can run like a river, quietly and sustainingly through life; it can be an intermittent sometime thing; or it can explode like a meteor, altering the atmosphere so that nothing ever feels or looks the same again.

> Molly Haskell
> American critic

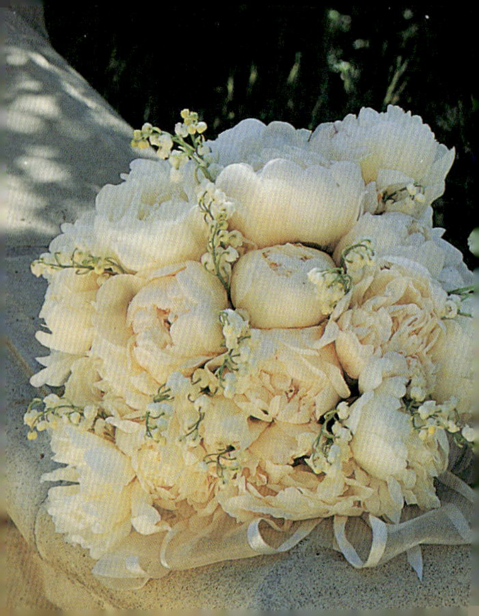

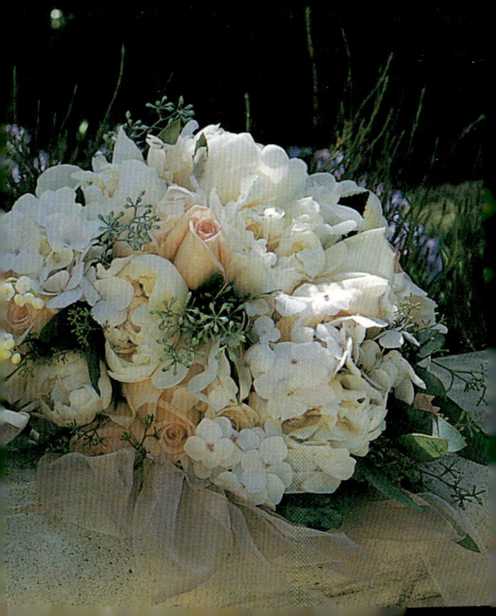

The bride, when she invites her relatives or friends to attend her, is saying that they are special to her. They, in turn, form a warm circle of friendship around the bride....

> Yetta Fisher Gruen
> American writer

If you never needed your girlfriends before, you need them now, if for no other reason than to keep you sane and perhaps even laughing.

Carmen Renee Berry and Tamara Traeder
American writers

Your bridesmaids deserve a special party all their own. . . . A splendid luncheon, an afternoon tea, or an elegant dinner pary that includes spouses and dates will let them know how much you appreciate their efforts.

> Beverly Clark
> American wedding authority
> and writer

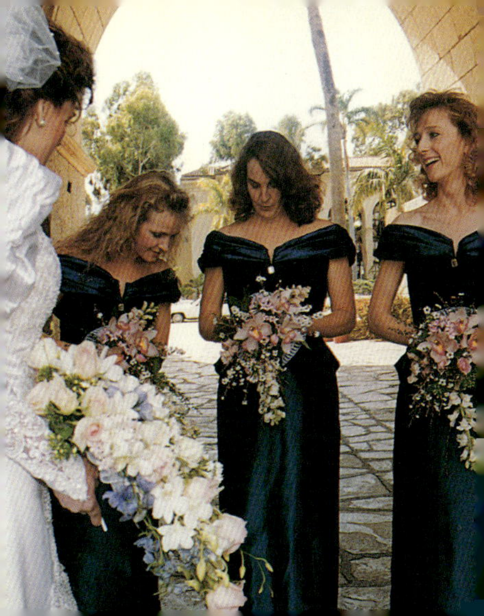

Full many maids clad
    in their best array,

In honor of the bride, come
    with their Flaskets,

Fill'd full of flowers, others
    in wicker baskets.

> William Browne (1591–1645)
> English poet

What happened with them made me happier, made my life better.

> Marilyn French
> American writer

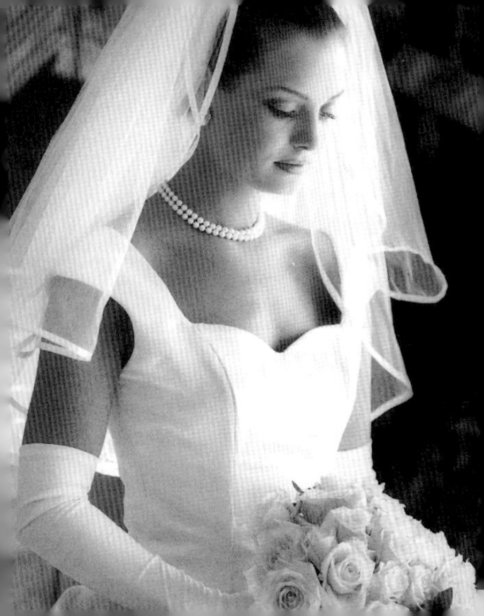

You have to laugh and cry over and over again with someone before you feel comfortable.

Joan Rivers
American comedian and writer

And what is laughter anyway?
Changing the angle of vision.
That is what you love a friend
for: the ability to change your
angle of vision, bring back your
best self when you feel worst,
remind you of your strengths
when you feel weak.

Erica Jong
American poet and writer

Happiness is a sunbeam which may pass through a thousand bosoms without losing a particle of its original ray; nay, when it strikes on a kindred heart, like the converged light on a mirror, it reflects itself with redoubled brightness. It is not perfected till it is shared.

                        Jane Porter
                    American writer

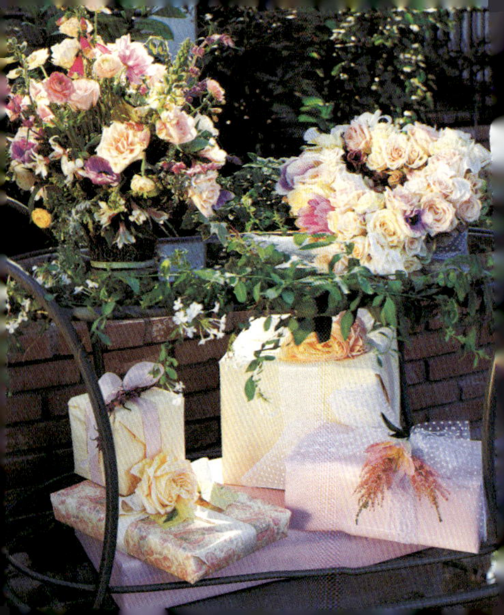

Unconditional Love

What I cannot love, I overlook. Is that real friendship?

Anaïs Nin (1903–1977)
French-born American writer

To want friendship is a great fault. Friendship ought to be a gratuitous joy, like the joys afforded by art, or life. . . .

> Simone Weil (1909–1943)
> French philosopher

Nearly every wedding album contains the classic portrait of the wedding party. Lined up, side by side with the bride and groom, smiling faces look out at us reflecting the joy in their hearts.

Arlene Hamilton Stewart
American writer

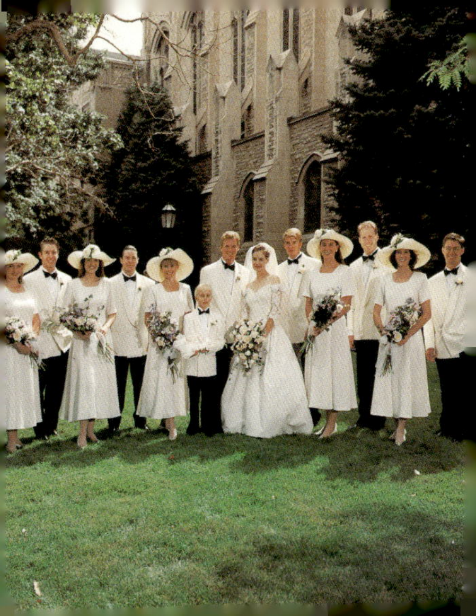

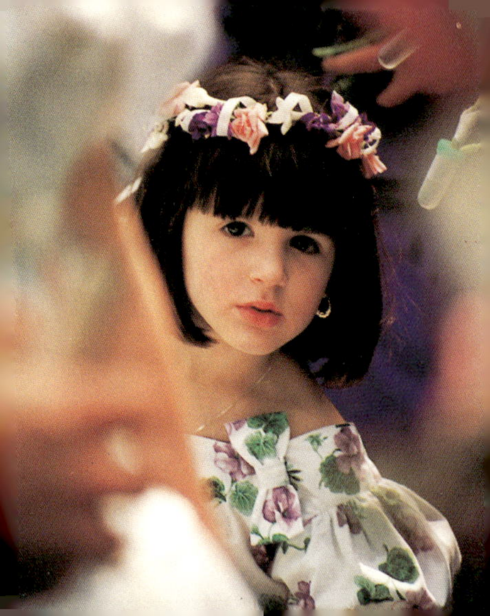

How can I find the shining word, the glowing phrase that tells all that your love has meant to me, all that your friendship spells? There is no word, no phrase for you on whom I so depend. All I can say to you is this, God bless you precious friend.

> Grace Noll Crowell
> American poet

Where there is great love
there are always miracles.

> Willa Cather (1876–1947)
> American writer

If you judge people, you have no time to love them.

Mother Teresa (1910–1997)
Founder, Missionaries of Charity

To love deeply in one direction
makes us more loving in all others.

Madame Swetchine (1782–1857)
Russian-born French writer

The openhearted and open-minded people are the strong ones.... They have the most power because they give instead of take. They give and gain while the losers take.

> Susan Trott
> American writer

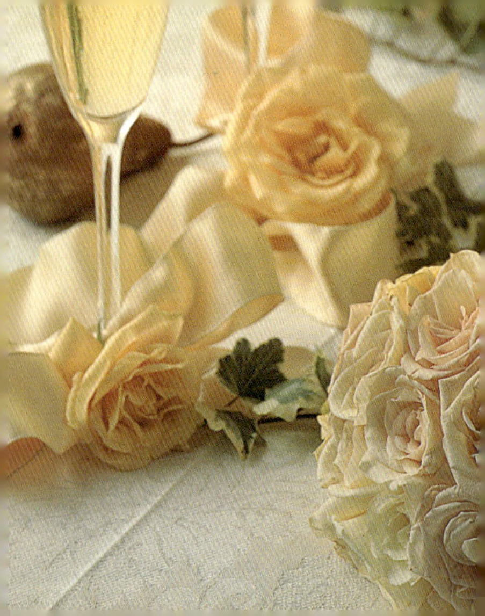

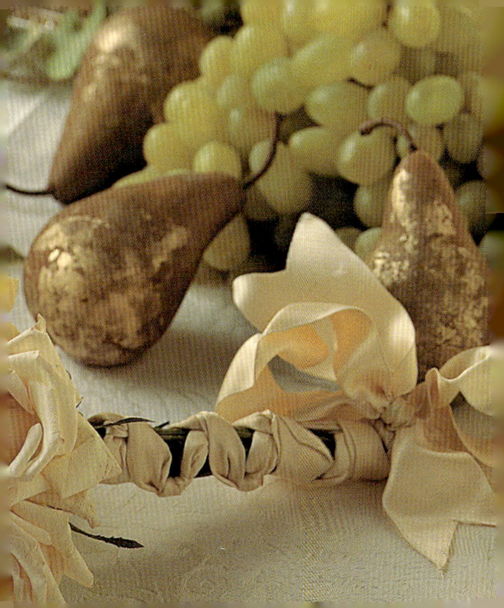

All you'll get from **stra**ngers is
surface pleasantry or **in**difference.
Only someone who **lov**es you will
criticize you.

> Judith Crist
> **Ame**rican film critic

A friend can tell you things you don't want to tell yourself.

> Frances Ward Weller
> American writer

A friend doesn't go on a diet because you are fat. A friend never defends a husband who gets his wife an electric skillet for her birthday. A friend will tell you she saw your old boyfriend—and he's a priest.

              Erma Bombeck (1923–1996)
                   American writer

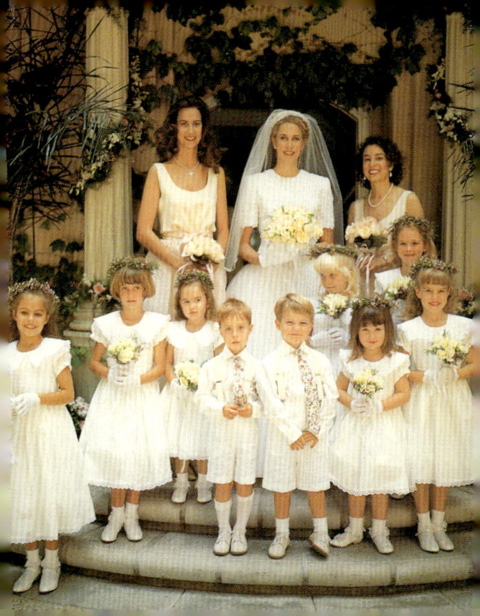

Love and friendship are profoundly personal, selfish values ... an expression and assertion of self-esteem, a response to one's own values in the person of another.

Ayn Rand (1905–1982)
Russian-born American writer

Life is a chronicle of friendship. Friends create the world anew each day. Without their loving care, courage would not suffice to keep hearts strong for life.

Helen Keller (1880–1968)
American writer and lecturer

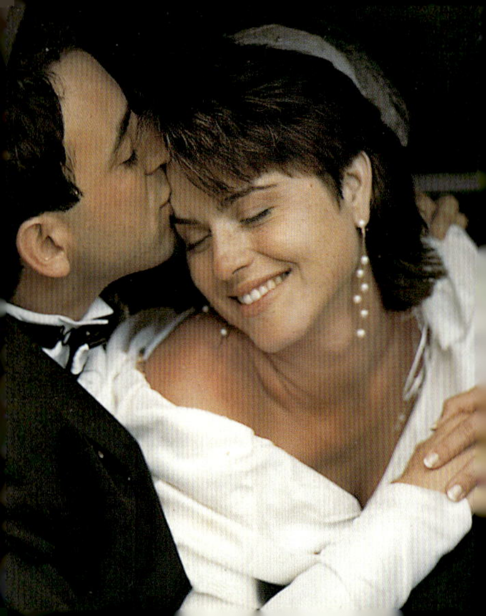

What do we live for, if it is not to
make life less difficult for each other.

>George Eliot
>[Mary Ann Evans] (1819–1880)
>English writer

It's the friends you can call up
at 4 a.m. that matter.

> Marlene Dietrich (1901–1992)
> German-born American actress
> and singer

The best relief from life was the presence of a friend who seldom asked for more than we could give.

> Barbara Raskin
> American writer

Friends seem to be like aspirin: we don't really know why they make a sick person feel better but they do.

> Letty Cottin Pogrebin
> American writer

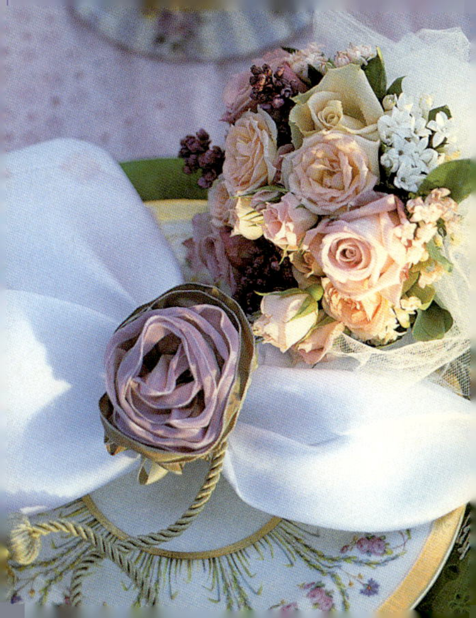

In times of trouble, your bridesmaids remind you of the love that brought you and your husband together and of your vows in the sight of God.

Martha Woodham
American writer

Does that mean I never let her down? Does that mean the rhythm is always in step? It means that in spite of, or including these issues, I absolutely can count on her. And what is so valuable is that I don't believe that is open to question.

> Catherine Smith
> American writer

When the wedding march sounds the resolute approach, the clock no longer ticks, it tolls the hour.... The figures in the aisle are no longer individuals, they symbolize the human race.

> Anne Morrow Lindbergh
> American aviator and writer

Soul-friendships are the
safety net of the heart.

> Susan Jeffers
> American lecturer

> If I don't have friends,
> then I ain't got nothin'.
>
> Billie Holiday (1915–1959)
> American singer

Photography credits

Amadeo: pp. 11, 108
 (courtesy of *Flowers & Magazine*)
Clay Blackmore: p. 100
Monte Clay: p. 68
Michael Garland: pp. 22, 65
C. Gregory Geiger: endpapers, p. 73
Calvin Hayes: pp. 30–31
Scott Hogue: p. 35
Kevin Hyde: p. 6
Brian Kramer: pp. 12–13, 32, 47, 92
Claudia Kunin: pp. 96, 112, 121
 (courtesy of *Romantic Homes* Magazine)
Madearis Photography Studio: pp. 42–43
Mark Papay: pp. 84–85, 89
Baron Erik Spafford: pp. 78, 102
Durango Steele: title page, pp. 16, 18,
 26–27, 49, 56–57, 116

This book has been bound using
handcraft methods and
Smyth-sewn to ensure durability.

The dust jacket and interior were
designed by Frances J. Soo Ping Chow.

The text was edited by
Elaine M. Bucher.

The text was set in Palace Script
and Weiss.